Guilt of Otherness

POEMS

Mohamed A. Eno

Published by
Adonis & Abbey Publishers Ltd
United Kingdom
P.O. Box 43418
London
SE11 4XZ
http://www.adonis-abbey.com

Nigeria:
No. 3, Akanu Ibiam Street.
Asokoro,
P.O. Box 1056, Abuja.

Year of Publication 2013.

Copyright © Mohamed A. Eno

British Library Cataloguing-in-Publication Data
A catalogue record for this book is available from the British Library

ISBN: 978-1-909112-36-0

The moral right of the author has been asserted

All rights reserved. No part of this book may be reproduced, stored in a retrieval system or transmitted at any time or by any means without the prior permission of the publisher

TABLE OF CONTENT

FOREWORD..VI
ACKNOWLEDGMENT..XIII
DEDICATION..XV
BACKGROUND...XVI
INTRODUCTION..17

Part I

A BRIEF PERSONAL MEMOIR..32

    The Bard's Parlance..35
    Somalia: A Nation So Egalitarian?...36
    The Stigma of Identity..37
    Memories of Otherness..38
    Otherness in the Classroom..39
    Ensconcing Identity..40
    Guilt of Otherness..41
    'A Shame to the Nation': Or a Shameful Nation?......................42
    Stings of Otherness..43
    "Don't Call the Outcast 'an Outcast'"..44
    Nobility Debased...45
    When the Outcast Is Adored..46
    From the Outcast's Diary...48

Part II

**THE DEBAUCHERY OF DICTATORIAL LEADERSHIP:
A DIARY**..49

    On Clan Vagrants...51
    Of Alien Eponym(s)...52
    From a Boatman to a Pedigree: A Somalo-Mythicology............53
    Clan Coronation..54
    Nation-Building: An Irony..55

The Nation: Eaters vs. Builders..56
Effigies of Tribalism..57
Blessed Revolution: Breadless Nation...58
The Social Interpretation of XHKS...59
From Camel Rustling to Aid Rustling..60
Clan Kiosks..61
"And Boots Too"...62
The Overnight Millionaire..63
The Lady of the Land Cruiser..64
Lamentations: A Forsaken Leader...65
Royal Reminiscences..66

Part III

LOSERS AND GAINERS: GLIMPSING AFRICA'S CIVIL WARS..67

War Sonnet..69
The Heartless..70
Armed for Booty..71
War Fantasy and Female Warlords..72
Exodus into the Wilderness..73
Killing a Close Kin..74
The Grave-looting Game..75
Kinship Loyalty..76
A Proud Killer..77
An Ill-fated Attack...78
"It Needs Bold Men Today!"..79
Confidential: From Mogadishu to Abidjan..................................81

Part IV

LEADERSHIP LOST: THE SOMALI TRANSITIONAL ADMINISTRATIONS..83

The Ideal Warlord!...85
Parliamentarian Pugilists..86
A Cult Called Clan Cabinet...87
Modern Minister's Confession...88

Kiosks, Coffee Shops, and Corner Garages.................................89
Today and Tomorrow...90

Part V

A LIMERICK ON LAME ACADEMIC LEADERSHIP.............91

The Poet: A Leader...93
Moral Decimation...94
Charlatans' Chicanery: A Poetic Barb......................................95
A Tactless Toady...96
The Incompetent...97
Nefarious Nexus...98
Pitiable Leadership: So Noxious a Premonition......................99
Disadvantage: Dichotomous Diction.....................................101
Till We Became Unseen..102
Reshuffles, Stunts, and Servants...103
Languish without Lament...104
Of Primates and the Boat: A Poetic Drama...........................105
A Call Too Desperate..106
The Sinking: May the Lord Save Sanura..............................107
The Unethical..108

Part VI

DIALOGUE OF THE DEAD...109

Arguments from the After-world: A Drama..........................111
The Unexpected Encounter...115

Part VII

A LIMN OF THE LOOTING SPREE: A PRESIDENTIAL DECREE...117

The Decreed Army Man..120
The Decreed Civil Servant..121
The Decreed Businessman 122
Prayers for the Decreed Incumbent.......................................123

FOREWORD

Mohamed A. Eno, a Kenyan poet, has added to the various East African poets' works. His first and recent poetry collection, *Corpses on the Menu: Blood, Bullets and Bones* (Outskirts Press, 2012), was a wonderful piece; but his second collection, *Guilt of Otherness*, is the subject of this foreword.

Let me begin with what some critics have suggested – that East Africa is suffering from creative barrenness. Nevertheless, with the advent of the poetry by Dr. Mohamed Eno, that statement seems to be successfully challenged if not proven implausible. Dr. Eno's poetry represents a beautiful corona amidst the earlier African poetry like *Poems from East Africa* (David Rubadiri and David Cook, 1971), *When Bullets Begin to Flower* (Margaret Dickinson, 1972), *Song of Lawino, Song of Ocol, Song of a Prisoner,* and *Song of Malaya* (Okot p'Bitek, various dates), *Boundless Voices: Poems from Kenya* (ed. Arthur I. Luvai, 1969), *Daughter of My People, Sing!* (Micere Mugo, 1976), *Tensions* (Richard Ntiru, 1971), *Drum Beat* (Leonard Okola, 1967), *Make It Sing and Other Poems* (Marjorie Oludhe Mcgoye,1995), *Orphan* (Okello Oculi, 1968), *Echoes Across the Valley* (eds. Arthur Luvai and Kwamchetsi Makokha, 2000), *A Study of the Poetry of Okot p'Bitek* (Monica Nalyaka Mweseli, 2004), *Imagination Of Poets*, (eds. Selina Onochie and Monica Mweseli, 2004), and *Womanic Verses* (eds. Marie Nelson and Monica Mweseli, 2008), just to name a few.

In particular, *Guilt of Otherness* combines onboard diverse realities about the poet Mohamed Eno's observation of the ills and evils in our world society today. It speaks of oppression of the marginalized, the questionable wealth of the illiterate, and of the violence meted to the "other," who represents the excellent one as exhibited in the poem bearing the very title of this illuminating collection:

Guilt of Otherness

The agony of being the *other*
Stings harsher outside school
As peers over half the class
Engage you in a battle
For answering accurately
A question they all missed.

Punches on the back head
Bitter blows on the face
More pounding in the belly
Bees of peers all over your body
Barrages of beastly kicks in your back
Bruises blown up on parts of your temple
Profuse gush of blood buries your face
Which now has puffed up brutally
To the size of a pyramid
Yet they brag at you:
Is it painful?

Eno's poetry does not miss to provide a critical observation of the leadership, the Head of State, who behaves as a colonial gatekeeper – that is, a character who is disconnected from the masses, his own citizens, and behaves as an anointed outsider who serves colonial objectives for his own gains, as sarcastically penned in the poem "Prayers for the Decreed Incumbent":

May the public remain blinkered
To the incumbent's predilections –
Amen!
May his ingenuousness
Endure him as Italy's blessed puppet –
Amen!

May the Bantu-Jareer be oppressed
Alongside the Yibir and Tumaal
As expressionless humans
Invalidated, incapacitated forever –
Amen!
May the learned stay numb
Over the entirety of his undoing –
Amen!
May his progeny benefit plenty
From pro-colonial *Borsa di Studio** –
Amen!
May his in-laws emerge blameless
Over the oft played-down *Leylkase* plot –
Amen! Amen! Amen!
May the expropriated Bantu Jareer land
He *inherited* from his colonialist colleagues
Enjoy nationwide legitimacy –
Amen! Amen! Amen!
May every *hal xaaraan* stolen she-camel*
Give birth to *nirig xalaal*/kosher calf –
Amen! Amen! Amen!
May we ordain him with affluence
In the annals of the national history
As the holy man unholy –
Amen! Amen! Amen!

* *Borsa di studio:* Italian phrase for scholarship grant

* From the Somali adage '*hal xaaraan ah nirig xalaal madhasho*' meaning – a stolen she-camel can never beget a *xalaal*/kosher calf.

With conciseness and rhythm, Mohamed Eno narrates the depth of his experiences in acerbic notes, namely that due to their subscription to colonial doctrine, the African leaders who replaced the Western colonizers just stepped in the latter's shoes. The poet therefore portrays the resultant mass conflicts; elite against elite, elite against poor, poor against poor, tribe against tribe, and finally even angels against perpetrators in a dramatic confrontation in the afterworld. He unravels, with care and sophistication, the anger, frustration, and rage evident of people all over the world (and Africa in particular) who still remain ethnically, socially, politically, and academically "in chains." The poet, in his creative work and critical view, makes his comprehensive social and political statement. Like Okot p'Bitek in "Song of Prisoner," the poet Eno's basic political views are that hopes of freedom have not been fulfilled, despite the virtual attainment of symbolic independence.

Furthermore, Eno points an accusing finger at scholars who compromise ethical balance in leadership issues or stay "numb" on the incumbents' weaknesses, or might euphorically accept their scholarship to serve as the leader's means to his own end. Consequently, he attempts to demonstrate in his poetry that the African people, including the academics, in post-independence times, are still frustrated, notwithstanding their being ruled by their own people. To display the societal resentment, Eno uses a variety of techniques to enhance the delivery of his message including irony, imagery, punctuation, experimentation, efficient vocabulary, narration, and experiential point of reality, among others. As such, he adds a passionate poetic voice to the continental outcry for an Africa that is liberated from the manacles of corruption, nepotism, discrimination, chaotic wars, and oppression. Employing verse as an effective vehicle of communication, the African poet airs the need to establish a platform for a genuine, more realistic African unity (*umoja wa ukweli*) in which citizens are equal both at the national as well as continental levels.

This collection is arranged into seven sections. In Part One, under the title *A Brief Personal Memoir*, Eno opens his lyrical discourse with what is presumably a cenotaph tracing of his childhood experiences. Here, as is also evident in other sections, he espouses vivid experiential account with lyrical creativity and sets out right with a beautiful note of appreciation to his teachers, followed by a poem, "The Bard's Parlance," where he quotes a traditional philosopher daring his colleagues over the quality and quantity of their contribution to the communal lore. From this very beginning, the poet

Eno is challenging us, the society, to unearth our hidden wounds through the power of the "Bard's Parlance" which, as the poet himself tells us, "reveals social dismay" that potentially "provokes the status quo." We don't need to ask further what happens to the powers that be once the foundation of their status quo has been "shaken." Besides that, the section discusses marginalization in a broad context, as well as the complexity of Somali identity from the inner circles of ethnocentrism and outcastism (in a nation most of the world believed to be egalitarian). With strong incantation, Mohamed Eno's poetry scrutinizes the concomitant roles certain local communities and colonial writers have played in creating distinctions among indigenous peoples they knew very little about; thus contributing massively to "the guilt of otherness" that robbed sectors of the African society of their citizenship rights.

Mohamed Eno mirrors the anomalies of post-independence Africa through the image of Somalia where Part Two focuses on the costly path of dictatorship as the few, including the most illiterate, enjoy luxurious life at the expense of the loyal nation-builders who continue suffering under the rule of corrupted and dictatorial regimes. He demonstrates this phenomenon in "The Overnight Millionaire" and "The Lady of the Land Cruiser" among other poems. Part Three sets its landmark on the senseless wars in the continent. It is also in this section that the poet presents two very peculiar and shocking scenarios: 1) that despite the massive atrocities due to poor governance, ethnic affiliation, anarchy, and clan ideology, the dead are yet very prone to losing their final resting home, the grave, to none other than deceased compatriots in what Eno poeticizes as "The Grave-looting Game"; 2) that more interesting in the section is how it develops a new contour in the war narrative by unraveling an often neglected trend: the negative role women play in armed conflicts, which the poet exposes under the headline "War Fantasy and Female Warlords." Eno concludes the segment by censuring the hypocritical nature of the International Criminal Court and the Western powers by setting a contrast between two categories of warlords: 1) those who stand to not only go scot-free with their war crimes but also gain financially from Western taxpayers' money, and 2) the *others* who are hunted down and arraigned for trial and conviction at the ICC – as the poet interpolates in the warlords' confessional statements "Confidential: From Abidjan to Mogadishu."

With six poems and a section prelude, Part Four wraps up the discussion of warlordism discussed in the preceding unit and is very critical of the failure of the Somali Transitional Federal Government whose approach of clan-based administration could not heal the nation's wounds, but instead went on a long self-serving journey of corruption and looting spree of public resources with no solution to the national impasse. Part Five embodies Eno's consciousness as a fervent participant observer of the world around him, digging into the fertile discrepancies within the academic world. Academia being the professional territory where his heart rests, the poet Eno portrays a plethora of traits that characterize poor academic leadership, disgust to neo-colonial elites, and incompetent academic leaders and administrators who resort to nepotism and favoritism in their bid to compromise the guiding ethics of academia. He writes satirically of the fate of dismay that awaits the unethical leader whose academic ethos suffers from the fractures of sound guidance and balanced wisdom. More specifically, it is in "Of Primates and the Boat: A Poetic Drama," that the East African poet informs the readers and stakeholders of the precarious ending to which poor academic leadership is doomed. To approach the subject from its complexity and justify his concern, Eno opens the section with a poem in praise of the social responsibility of the bard (meaning the intellectual or the academic); hence the necessity for scholars and those in academic leadership to give a keen ear to not only the poet's arguments but also, rather critically, to his predictions.

In Part Six, the poet Eno embarks on a fact finding mission to the hereafter. Here, he offers a presentation of a long dialogue (by eavesdrop?) between two former dictatorial leaders in recall of their miserable leadership in the first world and the repercussions they keep experiencing consequently in their eternal life. Part Seven closes the journey of Mohamed Eno's multi-thematic collection with a dramatic piece of poignant verse. It is in this concluding section that the East African bard eviscerates the rot at the incumbents' quarters in a sardonically worded, nerve-chilling form of prayers, as excerpted above in the title 'Prayers for the Decreed Incumbent'. A brilliant piece!

The poetry's vocabulary is accessible and hilarious, the experimentation in style is refreshing, and indeed the poet Eno is keeping the fire of African creativity burning by writing about urgent issues in the region, the continent, and the world over. In this volume, Dr. Eno inventively manipulates language and style in conundrum simultaneity, with an invocation of their coterminous relationship with social thought and environment. The poems, as discernible from the title, deal with the portrayal of stigma and pain as caused by various natures of marginalization, discrimination, hypocrisy, incompetent leadership, devastating wars, and poor governance, among other factors. With unique prudence, imagery, and foresight, the poet has added a very loud voice to the plight of the voiceless; he delivers a powerful message to the world to explore viable solutions for the deprivations laden to the social pandemics of marginalization, oppression, inequality, and injustice. With that motto, the poet believes, the world community will be able to finally address the anguish lived by the oppressed amongst us. This is a very informing, beautiful poetic excursion to experience and enjoy!

Alluta Continua!

>Monica Nalyaka Wanambisi Mweseli
>Professor of Literature, University of Nairobi, and Former Vice Chancellor, Kiriri Women's University of Science and Technology

ACKNOWLEDGMENT

It is at times too perplexing to record the names of all the contributors to a work, particularly if it had benefited from various supporters. Notwithstanding that, I would like to begin with my appreciation to the pair of scholars behind the sophistication of my literary as well as academic endeavor, my brothers Prof. Ali Jimale Ahmed and Prof. Omar A. Eno. With that tender tone of esteem, I don't need to mention that sister Batula and the extended family of *Adeer* Jimale Ahmed are naturally not just included but indeed very profoundly at heart, and for always. I thank Prof. Abdi M. Kusow and his family for always wishing me the best. Mohamud M. Afrah, my former editor-in-chief of Heegan Newspaper is commendable for his fairness, guidance and leadership.

I am pleased to acknowledge the comments and literary perceptions privileged to me by my colleagues at ADNOC Technical Institute (ATI), specifically Dr. Abdirizak Damak, Dr. Mohamed Azaza, Dr. Mubarak O. Taj Al Sir, and Mr. Ridwan Munir; their insights regarding comparative perspectives of both French and Arabian cultures is well adored. John F. Frymire, Markus Greutmann, Ahmednur Jama Adam, and Mr. Ali Al Maskari, thanks for being helpful whenever that was necessary. Very many thanks to Stephen Delaney for giving the manuscript a good shape in its initial editorial session; a wonderful job indeed! Mr. Ghalib Al Bir, my supervisor at the English Department, you are a wonderful expert, a true professional and a confident leader of class and quality, one every educator would like to follow his footpath. Mr. Nathan Leslie, thanks for your collaboration, especially for being there whenever the atmosphere seemed repellent, stubbornly nauseating.

For their ceaseless inspiration over the years, it is my delight to thank the extended family of *Adeer* Isse Karish, including the newly celebrated family of Mohamed A. Mohamud (Mohamed Gaaboow) and my beloved niece and former student, Hana Muse Ali. I wish you *wiil iyo caano, ubad suuban, kalgacal aan gaagixin, iyo bashbash iyo barwaaqo xag Eebbe ka yimid inaad ku waartaan* - Aamiin. Mr. Hassan Hanford of the ATI has accorded me a great deal of openness during our various discussions surrounding African American history and literary life; as such, I sincerely appreciate scholar Hanford's critical reflection of this work as an invaluable input. To the administrative team and colleagues at St Clements University Somalia and the extended family of St Clements Education Group go big thanks for their motivation and superb scholarship. Equally, my appreciation is due to Mr. Habib Souissi (Abu Writing), Abulqassim Abdulwahab, and all the rest of my colleagues and friends at the ATI, and of course my students across the continents.

My parents, Hagi Abdulakdir Eno and Hagia Halima Hussein Hassan (the best parents ever!) have a special place in my heart. They deserve even much more for being farsighted and inspirational, for being there for us whenever the destructive stigma of otherness bit on us deeper in the academic as well as other social situations. Their teaching of the values and moral strength in resisting against submissiveness and submission to oppression has contributed a lot towards the realization of our aspiration while growing up in a society so fraught with an inundated nature of severe otherization. The extended families of my brothers and sisters in various continents deserve a special admiration too, in a few words but extensively in affection, respect and value.

Ali Mohamud Osman (Caleey), Mohamed Yacub of WFP Somalia, and minority rights advocate and scholar Dr. Rasheed Farah, scholar Mohamed Hagi Ingiriis and their families have constantly assured me of their support, and I remain endlessly grateful. My family, from Cinta to Ramadhan alias Darel, have been supportive all the way and I thank them for their incessant love and motivation. Prof. Justus K. Makokha of Kenyatta University has motivated me in more ways than I could ever think of, and it is to that effect that I acknowledge my appreciation. Last but not least, the staff at Adonis & Abbey Publishers, you have done more than I expected and you certainly deserve my respect and gratitude for your professional approach, outstanding advice and editorial work. In fact, all those not mentioned, please accept my assurance that I am very proud of your contribution – with the deepest of humility.

DEDICATION

To all the men and women anywhere in the world who have undergone and/or resisted against any form of discrimination, marginalization, stigma and oppression, as well as the wise men and women in any society who have in one way or the other contributed to the fight against the evils in our human society in the forms of oppression, alienation and otherization of any nature, in any context and environment.

BACKGROUND

This project has come to birth because of Prof. Ali J. Ahmed's mentoring. His continuously encouraging words "Let the world hear you" extended the focus to a more engaging perspective: "Why don't you write a memoir?" Ahmed's words were so inspiring that they made the dim light at the end of the tunnel so bright, the long journey too short to cover, and the entire project nothing but stimulating. Therefore, in order to appreciate the Professor's encouragement, I had to undertake a project that responded to the issue from two fronts: a) a volume that had the reflection of a 'memoir', an account of experiences as lived and learned; and b) one which at the same time appealed to our (Ali and I) literary food for thought: poetry. Accordingly, I started the project with the title *Guilt of Otherness* and subtitle '*A Brief Personal Memoir in Poetry*', which categorically interprets the impact of *otherness* as seen and/or experienced in various contexts and across diverse stages of my life. However, when the work reached final stages, the publisher and Prof. Ahmed advised on dropping the subtitle from the front cover. Significantly, this work coincided with other projects that were ongoing as individual as well as collaborative works. The manuscript was ready by mid 2012, immediately after the completion of my first poetry collection *Corpses on the Menu: Blood, Bullets and Bones;* but again it was Prof. Ahmed's suggestion to push *Guilt of Otherness* to around mid 2013, in order to avoid a clash between the two volumes. It worked really well.

INTRODUCTION

Memories of Otherness!

Like a dwarf in a world of menacing giants, he [the otherized child] cannot fight on equal terms. — Allport (1954:139)

Discussing past societal evils such as inequality, marginalization and oppression experienced at early age takes you to a hideous memorial archive of what have for a long duration been masses of unhealed, torturous psychological wounds. The unforgettable emotional experiences remain so vivid that the wounds keep suppurating recurrently with incurable devastation, mentally and in many ways emotionally. Negotiating your means of survival in a hostile environment, where you are so easily prone to the teacher's punishment after you seek his/her recourse from your peers' bullying, taunting, degrading and physical abuse, makes your world not just a miserable space of earthly hell but a place not worth living in. When that space which represents the 'home of knowledge', the very centre designed to mold, shape, develop and produce an empowered future generation, concurs with the tyranny of ethnic segregation rather than incubate academic performance, it leaves a tainted mark in the memory of the *otherized* young victim. All this tragedy of otherness and exclusion, with its tormenting degrees and varieties of anguish, has left a recurring impact on me to this very date.

It is worthwhile mentioning at this point that, for some reason, after we had passed our entry test to the first grade, my father summoned us (me and my older brother Sayid-Ali) for an orientation. He, together with my mother, gave us a sincere prediction of the unavoidable circumstances of open marginalization, physical assault, psychological torture, and other kinds of hatred that lay ahead in our academic path. The advice was that we had to determine between submissiveness to the situation or resistance to any form of degradation. As we learned to hit back violently at aggressive peers from diverse ethnic backgrounds, we won a hard earned respect and some peace in the school environment.

However, our hard-won victories were undermined by the actions of some grown-ups or the insouciance of some teachers. To this day,

I'm haunted by our Math teacher and popular singer Mohamed Mooge's continuous repetition of the racial epithet *"reer tima adag"* (those of the kinky hair, or Africans) in class, during my fifth or sixth grade at Hodan Intermediate School. The teacher's words, in essence a not-so innocuous race-baiting, incited a few Northern female classmates from *Casa Popolare* area to follow suit even after he had left the school a very short while later. The legacy he left was awfully enduring, harsh in nature, psychologically traumatizing and academically demoralizing. It was only after my sister engaged two of the females in a bloody battle and we were summoned at the police station that I got some sort of relief from their uncouth tongue. Despite Mooge and a section of educators or artists of his thinking, I had some good quality teachers like Ustad Ibrahim, Mohamed Hagi, Alwan Hagi Hussein, Shamsa Abdillahi, Faduma Ahmed, Abdiaziz Hosh, Said 'the Djiboutian', Farah 'Dacas', and others during the critical period of my early years of education in Hodan, Casa Popolare and Hawl Wadaag elementary and intermediate schools. School principals like Sheikh Muse 'Ileey', Ahmed Geddi, Adan Omaar and Abdalla Ali Murshid alias Ustad Abdalow, were nice leaders who always endeavored to manage volatile situations in very modest and professional manner.

Demonstrating our worth among our elementary student community in the school environment (at a time when certain scholars still praise the state administrations in the sixties as 'democratic') was one thing; 'liberating' ourselves along the route we took to and from school was quite a different thing. For some time, we were targeted and harassed again and again for no other reason than 'belonging to Jomo Kenyatta'. The connotation here bears more weight and is tied much deeper to ethnic background in the sense that we were seen to belong to Jomo Kenyatta, a Bantu Jareer Kenyan. That 'Jomo Kenyatta' identity (being Kenyan or African) was employed as a good case to deny us the respect and rights we deserved. In the eyes of the perpetrators, we were *others*, outright aliens from another land; with less human dignity than the rest. The reason for our alienation and degradation was, as Somalist scholars who studied the Bantu Jareer factor in Somalia would later discover, that due to some peculiar reason, the 'noble'-claiming nomadic Somalis consider every black African inferior to the Somali. Moreover, it reflects the Somali belief that degrades every black African, regardless of his/her social status, education, intelligence or dignity, to slave status as long as that

African has s big nose, dark skin pigmentation and hard hair. According to those apocryphally constituted calibrations, we became regular objects of hate to the extent that even our sharing of the forms in the classroom, the classroom itself, or even the street was something many considered as unbecoming, totally unacceptable.

At Sudan Interior Mission, an English language private institution run by the American Peace Corps, I had some very nasty experiences. Here, whenever I answered a question, older boys sitting behind me pinched my ear time after time to distract me and/or force me out of the school. My books were either stolen or grabbed from me and torn into pieces because, to those boys, it was unpalatable that an *adoon*, or a Bantu Jareer (slave) could do better than them in learning a foreign language. But I had a deeper conviction and greater lust for learning than their jealousy could disenfranchise my young mind. I thanked God when the teacher saw the problem one evening and put me at the front chair, away from them and close to the blackboard. Later, my father had to come to the school and launch a complaint and explain the problem from an ethnic point of view. I was not only transferred from the class but I was also allowed to sit for a qualifying test to move to an upper level than my distracters. Consequently, my father arranged for me a means of transport as a safer way to reach home after classes. Even then, the problem didn't stop until one evening my brothers Omar and Sayid Ali and my sister Amina came for a battle; the kind of engagement one would call in Kiswahili '*kufa na kupona*' (to die and be relieved). A week or so from that night, I could walk home with less fear and anxiety. But it had to come with the cost of spilling precious blood from both sides, leading to police intervention and the American school teachers (not students) giving witness in my favor.

In my other private school study, mainly in the morning hours or during holidays, Hodan National School run by Adan Omaar, was a good experience, although I had to resist initial pressure by the students and prejudice by a few of the teaching staff. It was only after I had proved my point in performance that I became one of Omaar's favorite pupils, felt easing of pressure from class and school mates and also received some fairness in attitude from the other teachers. These squabbles in Mogadishu persuaded my parents to enrol me in Shabelle Secondary School in the agricultural town of Jowhar, about 92kms from the capital, a school managed at the time by the American

Mennonite Mission. The school was later nationalized by the military regime, but allowed to retain its U.S. curriculum along with its American teachers.

Here the environment was somewhat better, but once in a while the language and attitude of some of the students were emitting unmistakeable reflections of hatred and *otherness,* in the dorm, in the dining hall and at the sports ground. In one of several instances, one Thursday afternoon, while we were playing football in the fenced basketball court, I was wrongfully encountered by an older mate but in a lower grade, O. H., simply because I aborted several of his attempts to go past me and score. Students on his team/side blamed him for his being stopped by a 'Hawash', (an inferior Jareer) as some admitted to a schoolmate, Mohamed Abdullahi Addow, after the match. The next thing I knew was blows flying at me. I responded in a wild counteroffensive, despite his huge physique. When I was about to wrestle him down, Mohamed Abdullahi Addow, the oldest of the three Addow brothers moved in to separate us. He also gave a very severe warning to O.H., saying, "If you dare touch him again, it will be between you and me." That support from Addow was quite a sigh of relief, although I had to prove to the cynics and stigmatizers, those with pastoral mental incapability in understanding human equality and dignity that I did well whatever I participated in, be it curricular or extra-curricular activities. This was quite a good experience though, and somehow better than the continuous fighting my brother and I had experienced in Mogadishu. My brother Sayid-Ali was at the time in a boarding school in Baidoa, about 250 km away from the capital and roughly 350 km from my school town of Jowhar.

When I joined college, I started looking at the society from different perspectives. With professional certificates in Journalism and Writing from the British Tutorial College, Nairobi, Kenya, I had a good standing for exemptions at the College of Education to complete a Bachelors Degree majoring in English. Later, I couldn't secure permanent recruitment so I started assisting my father at the farm until I started working part time for Heegan Newspaper, where I had been working unpaid for some time and despite a hard effort by the editor-in-chief, Mohamud Mohamed Afrah for my recruitment. I later got part time jobs at the English Department of the Somali National University and at the Technical and Commercial Teachers Institute known as the Polytechnic.

Elsewhere in my first volume of essays, *The Bantu Jareer Somalis: Unearthing Apartheid in the Horn of Africa*, and in verse form in this volume, I described how our neighbor was overcome by envy upon seeing us immaculately dressed in our uniform and heading to school. She told my mother how it was a waste of time educating us when indeed it was obvious that we wouldn't be employed by the state at any level, given our ethnic Bantu Jareer background. I also provided, as have several other scholars done, a clear description in prose and poetry of the political alienation, social discrimination and economic marginalization impacted on this segment of the society. Needless to say, the plethora of derogatory epithets, hatred and degradation flies in the face of the oft-quoted Lewisian doctrine of Somali homogeneity, pastoral democracy or egalitarian society in the Horn of Africa; descriptions presented subjectively but also inappropriately.

Blinkers and Twisters in Somali Scholarship

Nin dhiigaayo gadaashiis, nin dhinti ka daymoo.
Behind the bleeding one (of your kinfolk) could be a dead one (of the other kinship).

Although a good corpus of literature exists on the prevalence in Somalia of a very rigid caste system, severe forms of ethnic marginalization and proven physical evidence to that effect, the post colonial administrations and the treacherous proponents of the self-same political agenda have done everything in their power, from politics to the pen, to obscure the multiethnic and multicultural reality about the country. The manipulation encumbered all forms of scholarship save that which heaped encomia on pastoralism and its camel complex. The notion was tantamount to a state-purported scheme that was utilized as a socio-political device to suppress and oppress, in simultaneity, the culture as well as existence (among other communities) of the Bantu Jareer section of the society. It was, furthermore, in tandem with the societal campaign that hinges on the principle of supremacization of the pastoral nomad who claims Arab ancestry as compared to the inferiorization of the Bantu Jareer as a claimant of his African descent.

From the grim reality of such gruesome background (see more in M. Eno 2008), I would like to correct Professor Lidwien Kapteijns's unfounded and profoundly spurious assertion: "Socially discriminated, they [the Bantu Jareer community] nevertheless enjoyed considerable political and economic opportunity in post-independence Somalia" (2013:271 note 136). Kapteijns' new discourse into the Somali studies is not just shockingly outrageous but in fact academically disappointing, if not at all mythically exaggerated and wantonly misinformed. Yet, without contributing any credible evidence to corroborate her statement, Kapteijns dispatches a powerfully misleading assertion of Bantu Jareer enjoying a 'considerable...opportunity' in the Horn of Africa!

On the contrary, and specifically starting from the post-independence period of the so-called democratic administrations down to the end of the military dictatorship of Siad Barre, neither can Professor Kapteijns nor any of her dubious informers provide the name of just one single Bantu Jareer army general, minister, permanent secretary, director general, ambassador, or general manager. Kapteijns' bold but reckless allegation is not corroborated by empirical reality upon which the reader can draw factual findings. Had she done her homework with some diligence, she would have realized that no field researcher nor, for that matter, Somali society at large, have witnessed a Bantu Jareer benefiting from investment loans, agricultural development funds, scholarships and education grants, land grabbing, nor any other opportunity for development. This pithless discrepancy renders a serious flaw in her basic conceptualization of the very problem under her scrutiny. It is a flaw that would ultimately cast aspersions on her overall 'clan-cleansing' project.

Credible field studies/research conducted by serious Somalia scholars and Bantu Jareer social memory, reveal how these communities have experienced nothing except being victims of ethnic-based economic cleansing, ethno-political cleansing, ethnic up-rooting as well as being recipients of all sorts of hate discourse and discrimination. Ironically, much of this scholarship was/is available to all scholars, including Kapteijns. That said, it would be very useful, for the sake of academic debate and discussion, if Kapteijns could identify the source of her information or the outcome of her empirical research in order to share with the rest of scholarship the epistemological facts that inform her arguments about the Bantu Jareer. In any case, Kapteijns' conjecture invites the poetic allusion of whether one can merely twist at will a theme whose details and possible trajectories one clearly lacks:

Gableey (shimbir) ma gashaa gariir gogoshiisa?
Gamuun gana weenaa guf laaga dhigaa

The degree of fallacy contained in her malicious statement delivers Kapteijns absolutely out of touch with the undercurrents and crosscurrents of what constitutes ethnic marginalization and ethnic cleansing (as compared to her apocryphal 'clan cleansing'). Her lack of knowledge of the Bantu Jareer community veritably lays open Kapteijns' narrower scope of Somali studies than her measly 'clan cleansing' project deems the focus on, for whatever reason. By further observing the work in general, one cannot help but stumble on Kapteijns' struggle in the mist of clan relations in Somalia as exhibited in her lack of clarity and inability to disentangle between the Reewing-Digil-Mirifle constituents and the Bantu Jareer community on the one hand, and the Bantu Jareer within that confederation's cluster of communities on the other (a study to shed light on the origins of such lacunae is underway). Suffice it to say, Kapteijns' 'clan-cleansing' reveals the scholar's blind spots as she egregiously misrepresents the Bantu Jareer condition in Somalia. Apparently, her exaggerated bias and intentions to pave the way for the subjects of her 'clan cleansing' project to be seen as 'victims' runs counter to the reading of the situation by those of us (at the time I was editor-in-chief of Banadir Newspaper) who witnessed the dynamics of the unfolding events of the Daarood-Hawiye or Hawiye-Hawiye (Mahdi vs. Aideed) wars of 1991-1992 and beyond.

By contaminating her work with what certain scholars would term as "intellectual contraband" (Grigorian, 2007:186), Kapteijns must have perceived that the best method (without supporting field research) to justify a case for yesterday's oppressors to assume (alongside the Bantu Jareer) a position as today's victims of 'clan cleansing' (Kapteijns' academicized fabrication) was for her to somehow layoff conventional knowledge far back in this context. Therefore, by transforming a beaten armed warrior into a civilian victim (at least in her writing), she would then dismiss existing scholarship that reveals the vicious atrocities of discrimination, hatred, and stigma, which her supposedly *cleansed clan* had been perpetrating not only against the Bantu Jareer people but by extension against the whole country and in distinct modes; from pre-colonial period through post-independence as well as during the current situation of anarchy, to introduce just a tip of the iceberg (consult *'Libro Verde' doc. 2, p.27 – communication between Filonardi in Zanzibar and Crispi, then Italian Prime Minister; Robin Hallet, 1999:130, 131; 'Libro Verde', doc. 11, annex 1, p.40 – Treaty of Protection; ASMAI, pos. 59/1, f.8 – communication between Lunay in Berlin, Germany, and Crispi, March 1889; ASMAI, pos. 59/1, f.5 – containing Yusuf Ali's declaration in Alula in April 1889; 'Libro Verde', doc. 29, annex II, p.69;* Douglas Collins 1960; Ahmed 1996; Besteman 1999; Mariam A. Gassim 2002; O. Eno 2004; Abdulahi Osman 2007; M. Eno 2008; BRT Somalia 1995; Martin Hill 2010; Mohamed Ingiriis 2012; A. Kusow & M. Eno forthcoming).

The concern thus remains, when academics suffocate the truth about Bantu Jareer oppression by overriding all the literature available, and most recently the US sponsorship of the Bantu for resettlement at a staggering number of about 14,000 people, one would be enticed to join in Kapteijns' circus of theatrical satire, if only for the sake of illuminating the *fadhi-ku-dirir* stance chosen by the scholar, though not worthy slithering off the academic ladder with her. For, from an analytical point of view, Kapteijns' accounts on the Bantu Jareer need no further interpretation than classify them within the domain of hatred, hate narrative and denial of academic facticity, despite her accusation of the same on others. But facts should be untapped in their consistent manner, and sometimes by engaging the communal lore that sets the premise of our social culture:

Gani ii gabalaaloow gaanjiwaa taqaan
Gambaalo ad gaarin see ku guntaheey?

Gabalaalow (classic design) gold jewellery is for high life females
How dare one dress (haut couture) *gambaalo* one is yet to attain the class?

This is to reveal that, from the outset, Kapteijns contradicts herself (as she does throughout the work in concern) by first describing the Bantu Jareer as 'socially discriminated' before adding in a quick glimpse that they also benefited from 'considerable' advantages. Here again, and in line with the mist and inconsistencies I mentioned above, one wonders how a research scholar would be oblivious of the paradigmaticality that a 'socially discriminated' community has, by that act of discrimination, automatically been excluded from existing opportunities; and that one in that kind of social oppression would not perform on equal platform with his oppressor who is simultaneously the composer and conductor of the discrimination orchestra. However, evasiveness from accuracy, (not to mention academic factuality) seems to have created self-obstruction to Kapteijns, especially her potential to explain how in the Somali context a community excluded as the *other* could at the same time be offered 'considerable' opportunities by the same proponents who are also the creators and corporate leaders of the exclusion enterprise. Worse even, Kapteijns' hypothesis regarding 'considerable...opportunity' to the Jareer suffers from lack of necessary supporting evidence that might help it hold its firm ground to disprove the conventional version suggesting the oppression and ethnic discrimination the community has been entangled with.

With that uncorroborated note, and regardless of any intrinsic or extrinsic motives, a devastating compromise of academic credibility is evident in the chronicling of *sheeko-xariir*-like concoctions of myths and trails of inaccurately conceived and consumed datum of whatever kind. Needless to suggest the informants constitute the affiliates and affinities of the very core players who consciously wrecked the country into the mayhem, drained state coffers, sucked the blood of the hardworking citizens (read also M. Eno, 2012, *Corpses on the Menu*), but who for some time now have been striving to switch position as victims. They have been desperate to attain the position to the extent that they could utilize every possible means, from mean propaganda to the nib of those not deeply conscious of the ethno-political conundrums locked in the underbelly of the Somali society in its holistic nature. The enormity of such manipulation is luminous from the '*clan cleansing*' work itself that the selected informants were crafty enough to capitalize mainly on the information gap in the part of the researcher; particularly the investigator's lack of analyticality to sift through the idealistic account offered and the realistic environment that she vehemently compromised. Additionally, they provided her with half-baked data supported by their knowledge of the researcher's limitations concerning her lack of fieldwork information, thus apparently exploiting the constriction.

Professor Kapteijns' study reminds us of earlier studies about the southern Somalia communities in general and the Bantu Jareer in particular, where they have been victims of misleading and utterly biased academic works whose authors had neither set foot in the area they were investigating nor had any contact with the communities they claimed to have studied and become authority on. If Lewis was blamed yesterday as a 'colonial writer' (and to some degree a 'racist') serving the purpose of his nation and its interests, *'Clan Cleansing'* has been devised as a clear clan mouthpiece through which dishonest diasporic informants attempt to conceal their culpability in the role they played in the national impasse. By far, though, the work is so shy of demonstrating relevant field study to support the contextual assertions it tends to mitigate about the multi-layered deprivations of the Bantu Jareer people to whom Kapteijns refers collectively as slaves from parts of Africa, thereby denting the historian's ethics in approaching the subject from its multi-diagonal spheres. The conspicuous elements of compromise on the one part, and the mythical nature of the study on the other, give a reason for the bard to an accusing finger at the culprit:

Been ku baytamoow ninkii besi waayo
Banaan bood leheenaan baal laaga tifaa

The necessitation is urged partly by the academicization of the fallacies Kapteijns has smeared against the Bantu which, in turn, entices not only a redirecting of the truth in its right course, but indeed as a message to the producer about people's awareness, lest the reappraisal of the consequences of the discrepancies is orderly placed for future consciousness of her work. In effect, the contention derives from the reality that according to factual academic paradigm, a work whose pillars were built on the foundation of irrelevant (know-all) informant unrelated to the theme, only contaminates the essence of the study in its material and moral value in both validity as well as reliability, internally much so as it spreads the contamination externally.

My contention here suggests that the categorical distinction between the fieldwork approach and the *third party* approach can be gleaned from the quality of the works of the scholars who conducted their inquiry in the respective areas in the country and those from the mindset of simplistic hearsay paradigm of scholarship. In other words, those who seek 'authority' status through affinities, affiliations and short-cuts do not in any way deserve comparability to the researchers who based their investigation on participation; by taking that academically daring extra mile of living with the community, and accessing their sentiments and emotions in the context of their day-to-day life. The latter category of scholars avail themselves to the opportunity of acquiring firsthand information from the subjects themselves, thereby accessing the communal culture and life as experienced in their natural undertaking. Relatively, the poet's classification of the two types of scholars reflectively ensues, as explained in the couplets below:

Buug baani-hawaas (lee) ma loo barahaayo
Besteman bur sooraay Bantu la cuneeysi!

That learning (about a community) does not occur in vacuum (is true of)
Besteman who has surely lived the Bantu culture and philosophy of life

Bilaajo nin gaarin Buufoow agahiis
Bal ganleey ku taalaaw bariid u mudaa!

A researcher ignorant of the subjects of his study
Meets pitfalls of mistaking maize with rice (sullying his work)

Adoo bukureey bariito ku boowin
Bu'aalena gaarin buug see ku dhigeey?

How can one unfamiliar with a culture
Chronicle a volume about its community?

Since I sprinkled a few *shurub* couplets in Somali Bantu Jareer dialect of the environs of Afgoye, let me now take a brief poetic excursion into the Somali pastoral medium, one which the author of the work concerned in these few paragraphs might find it easy to decode:

Runta lama saluugo oo saani baa loo sare adkeeyaaye
Subac nin akhriyoo salaadi gabay janna hore usoo seegye
Sanado tagey nin suulayoo sibraarkii biyo daadshey
Wallee suus baad qooysatoo kaa sid weyn sarbeebti garanweyday
Siriq qabiil adaa ku sirmayoo siiri colaad kugu yeeray
Sabi la hasaawgi saq dhexe waa kaa ku sarjimeeyaye
Saangudubka soo kuma seejinin saldhiggii aqooneede?

The verse undergirds the fact that an unanalysed or haphazardly construed discourse of any nature bears the potential of portraying its author as a negligent victim of the author's very work, especially what pertains to ethnic studies in Somalia and more specifically the complexity of the Bantu Jareer factor whose study has been (and still is) a kind of taboo to Somali scholars. It further denotes how reckless oblivion to the biases of mono-dimensional informants can make an investigator treat a sensitive subject from the perspective of *rati-ishooli*, a one-eyed camel that grazes only from one side due to the burden of his disability.

In contrast, what the lyrical corpora in this collection reveal, and what experts (Eno & Eno 2010, 2009, 2007; Eno 2008; Lewis 2008; Ali 2004; Kusow 2004; Farah et al. 2002; Gassim 2002; Luling 2001; Besteman 1999, 1996,1991; Ahmed 1996, 1995; Cassanelli 1995, 1982; Menkhaus 1989) as well as relief agencies and human rights organizations (Hill 2010; Lehman and Eno 2003; BRT Somalia 1995) have written about the community in question, represent the broader context of the unfilled gaps that amount to the depreciation of the *'Clan Cleansing'* hamlet of narrative. Regardless, a more expressive incantation reflective of Somali Bantu Jareer dialect is also imbued here in its right order, if only for further invocation of the communal lore to bridge the lacuna:

Bileey-shalab hadiid naqatayood been lee ka badsaweeysi
Buugna ood ku qorati baas ma arkin Bantu Jareerweyne
Bandarki ood fidhisiyaad bi'isi boos aqoonyahaneedka
Baashaal hunkiis lee maad boqno-goos uskugu rideeysaa
Barshidhac adoo ku jiro amaa taxdi been wareerkaan

Concluding couplets:

Boog baarka ku taal maa baanteeda heleey
Buuta baarinkaada maxaad u berxeeysi?

Since you are unable to remedy a contagion in the liver
Oh Buuta! Wasn't it unworthy contaminating your learned status?

Buuy basiiradaa waakaa buriyeen
Been baalal leheen aay buug kuugu shuween

Oh Buuy! With those unfounded conjectures
They've surely dented your (academic) prowess

 Kapteijns' unanalyzed statement aside, the Bantu Jareer and the other oppressed ethnicities in Somalia, call them minorities or outcasts, have not had in their memory a harmonious living environment in the peninsula. At best, they have been (and still are) treated as second class citizens and, in many circumstances, as non-citizens, (Kusow 2004; Eno & Eno 2010). One need not look far for evidence as it is factually engrained in the 4.5 political power-sharing ideology of the country. A vast majority of so-called learned men and women with titles such as Dr, Prof., Avvocato (Lawyer), Sheikh, Ugaas, Suldaan, Culumaa'uddiin, Aqoonyahan (intellectual) have all in their entirety failed to consult their faculty of reasoning (if at all they had any over and above clanocracy) over the varied consequences of the Four-Point-Five pandemic to the image of the country, nationally and also internationally.
 To that extent, even a section of scholars (from the point of gain to their clan interests) procured this apartheidist segregation and oppression as a milestone, describing it a "famous 4.5 system", one which those with the internalized superior/inferior mentality saw as a

"victory" with "practical relevance" (A.M. Abdullahi [Baadiyoow] & I. Farah 2007). Yet others equated it to an "important achievement" (Mukhtar 2007), notwithstanding the fact that not only all of these are Muslims who should abide by the equality enshrined in the Islamic doctrine but, shockingly, that some are indeed specialists in Islamic Studies who should have been at the forefront of censuring the un-Islamic bond and anomaly inherent in the system! In effect, and apart from the exaggerated titles, the decision-makers of the segregationist, oppressive, degrading, derogatory and infamous Four-Point-Five (4.5) power sharing plague have in the most irresponsible manner demonstrated an enormous lack of wisdom, diabolical judgment, massive hatred, violent social marginalization, political ineptitude, and deeply entrenched moral impurity against the constituent enterprises of Islamic ethics and doctrine.

The Four-Point-Five debate and in general the issue of equality among citizens and their cultures has penetrated deeper into society that an opposing section of scholars raised the moral decadence laden to this exclusionist road map and denial of equal rights to the ethnically marginalized. Among the erudite who deprecated the contagious menace of segregation and in fact vigorously contested against its application include Abdi I. Samatar, Ali J. Ahmed, Ahmed I. Samatar, Omar A. Eno, Abdi M. Kusow, Mohamed A. Eno, Mohamed H. Ingiriis, Catherine Besteman, and ordinary citizens from all walks of life, who expressed their sentiments in forums and blogs on web sites as well as formal and informal gatherings. It is due to the enormity of the oppression and the willingness of the continuation of the epidemic by the section of society allergic to equality and human dignity, that this section is added as a clarification to Kapteijns' disheartening comment exhibited above.

To add insult to injury, some of the advocates of the Four-Point-Five system have expressed its irreversibility because it was the *only* way the delegates at that time and in that conference could craft a method on sharing power. This, sad and deplorable as it is, makes one pity the *indheergarad* (intelligentsia) and *aqoonyahan* (intellectuals) of a nation who could not devise a solution more just and appropriate than one in which they determined the legalization and constitutionalization of the debasement and discrimination of a very important sector of the society, mainly because (among other factors mentioned above) these marginalized communities did not participate in the insanity of looting public treasury and the ensuing atrocities of warlordism -- factors many short-sighted people consider as the yardstick for awarding accolades and accepting a clan's equality to others (see Eno & Eno 2009).

Part I

A Brief Personal Memoir

In appreciation of Moallim Abdulle Ali, alias Macallin Cabdulle Dheere, senior scholar of the Moallim Nuur Qur'anic and religious center (Moowlaca Macallin Nuur) at Suuqa Siigaale in Hodan District of Mogadishu, and the late Sheikh Hassan Suleen, both my Qur'anic teachers, and all the dedicated educators, men and women, from whom I learned formally or informally.

Edification prevails
In the essence of its being
When
In the memory it archives
Sequences of experiences
As
Nostalgic moments of facts
From which one retrieves
Very
Worthwhile resolutions
To engage with current quandaries
While
One arduously prefigures
The tussle with future challenges

The Bard's Parlance

Nimbo juunigiisaan soo jooji lahaay
Maxaa jib ka siiheey oo noo jiriheey?

If I may set for each bard a container (just to dare you)
What best thing would you fill it up with?
                    —Mohamed Ali (Weershe)
                    (My translation)

The potency of the bard lives in the parlance
The parlance is nurtured in the expressive mind
The expressive mind embodies vision
Vision transpires human desire
Desire becomes the host of reflection
Reflection mirrors inspiration
Inspiration triggers the drive in the soul
The soul relates reality to the mind
The mind transmits the bardic image
The bardic image entices the tongue
The tongue hurls the bardic parlance
The bardic parlance reveals social dismay
Social dismay provokes the status quo
Status quo provoked shakes its foundation
Foundation shaken informs disequilibrium
Disequilibrium denotes daunting dysfunction
Daunting dysfunction entices doom and destruction.

Somalia: A Nation So Egalitarian?

To the colonial writers and students of Somalia's mythical egalitarian doctrine.

And their confession was in daylight:
…So we anointed at midnight
The imperial anthropologist
With the egalitarian ideology:
We're all equal.
Though under the surface
Inequality was the agenda
We obsessively fed him with
From the potions we stirred.
No matter the off-track attributes
Or the inscriptions of egalitarianism
We have *others* forever among us
As he approved by the colonial ink.

Somalis are all equal
Of Arabian nobility
The *others* are not our equal
Due to their Africanity.
Nor are they of equal intelligence
To us, the pastoral democrats.

The Stigma of Identity

Oh, how painful the stigma
When they belittle the birthmark
The pride of the big nose
The particulars of the kink
Bristle that banes them
Or
When they vilify
Your aesthetic beauty
And punditry at the skills
The technological prowess
Bestowed upon you!

Oh, how painful the stigma
When they besmirch your being
To cover their absolute poverty
Of nature's beauty.

Memories of Otherness

Coming a little late on Saturday
Brings you to reality
With the "harsh stick of Saturday"
That knows not forgiving
Over errors minor
As minor as sleeping
Until the sun opened
Its face in the east.

How dearly you pay
With harsh flogging on Saturday
That devours your small body
For playing with peers on Friday –
That you may expect
A gift of extra flogs
When you are the *other*.

Otherness in the Classroom

Another strange world
This intimidating environment
Peopled by small creatures clad
In white and blue:
The symbol of the nation
As they say.

Steal a quick gaze to the right
A few keen lookers at you
Another gape to the left
All the way to your back
Eyes inquisitive
Yet alert on you:
A tale of their stunning experience
Of how you became among them
You who renders the atmosphere
Of their all-nobles classroom
Unholy, impure.

Ensconcing Identity

Unlike seeds
Are best sown apart;
Weeds shouldn't wither
A harvest well watered.

Falcons and fowls
Don't feature as same
Though all full of wings
Each flies unlike the other.

Distinct formulas apply
To Somali proper
And the Somali improper;
Though we're all humans
Not all of us are humans.
We are the humans
The *others* less humans.

Guilt of Otherness

The agony of being the *other*
Stings harsher outside the school
As peers over half the class
Engage you in a battle
For answering accurately
A question they all missed.

Punches on the back head
Bitter blows on the face
More pounding in the belly
Bees of peers all over your body
Barrages of beastly kicks in your back
Bruises blown up on parts of your temple
Profuse gush of blood buries your face
Which now has puffed up brutally
To the size of a pyramid
Yet they brag at you:
Is it painful?

'A Shame to the Nation': Or a Shameful Nation?

Every ornament in a house
Preserves its beauty
In its place at home;
Neither the mortar
Nor the pestle
Nor the sweeper
Nor the floor
Defers the duty
In its domestic function.

Loading books on children
Overburdened already with
The stigma of a broad nose
Assumes a mythical panacea
Of parents beleaguered
By wishful thinking
Against a state policy
That ignores low ethnicities.
For a noble approaching
A functionary of the ignoble
For assistance in a public office
Smears shame unto a nation
So ennobled in the literatures
Of colonial scholars.

Stings of Otherness

Oh! Look at them!
Look! What an irony!

Immaculate dressing we can't afford
Albeit our status above them
Invites a question enough genuine
About the ownership of this land.

Is it for us, the Somali offspring,
Or the *others* from Kenyatta land?
Either we engage them
In an endless fight
Or they take from
This route a flight.

Flight from a route
Embodies cowardice
Odd to our culture
Despite our *others* status;
Fighting all the way home
Became our practical option
Of the imminent engagements
Before it took an organized gang
To encounter us, the *others,*
Every day on our way to school.

"Don't Call the Outcast 'an Outcast'"

One whose string was severed
From its bond to the kinship
Survives in a tumultuous low life
A kinless untouchable, unwanted

He must have psychological stamina
To endure the pejorative epithets
We advance to acknowledge him of his
Outcasthood, as the unacceptable inferior

Even when our offspring insults
And the offended seeks redress
The inferiority epithet comes
Reaffirmed in the reproaches
To the offending child:
Don't call the outcast 'an outcast'!

Nobility Debased

Ina-Gob returns home
With bulging sweat
The size of African beads
Pouring from his face
Profusely all over his body
As he misses the bench
The wife placed for him.

She welcomed him with dismay
Her failure to secure funds
From the journeys to the kinship
Failing to fusion to life a kitchen
Now dead for the third day.

In a pragmatic nature the husband boasts:
I paid a visit to the *Tumaal* blacksmith
Who filled brand-new hundreds
Into my penniless pockets.

Negation of wealth from Allah
Negates me nothing as a noble
For the non-nobles next door
Have long been known to that narrative.

When the Outcast Is Adored

When the exam questions
Overwhelmed the entire class
Of the so-called nobility
And I worked out the answer
They called me Aboowe*
Not "the outcast".

When the opponents asked
For a soccer encounter
The nobility offered
No outstanding striker
And I took the day for them
They called me Aboowe
But not "the outcast".

When the educational competition
Of interscholastic achievement
Arose to its apex
And I bore the school torch high
They called me Aboowe
Not "the outcast".

After pulling victory
In every encounter
The outcast asserts:
Elevate me with endless applause
For ensconcing your interests
Until I'm again tomorrow
The same old outcast
Abused as the inhabitant of *Ureyso**

Notes

Aboowe: means respected older brother; it is the equivalent of the Kiswahili term *kaka*.

Ureyso: denotes stink, filth. It is also the name of an isolated slum in Hargeysa, capital of Somaliland, where the marginalized ethnicities live, lest they *contaminate* the so-called noble society. (See also M.A. Eno & A.M. Kusow "Racial and Caste Prejudice in Somalia" forthcoming.)

From the Outcast's Diary

They came in the land
Scaring skeletons, undressed
Ignorant in the art of survival
By average well under
Our living intelligence.

We embraced, humanized
Enshrined, anointed
Incorporated them
Into our royal cult
As equals among us.

When a ferocious foe from
Across the seas attacked us
We engaged them with spreads
Of arrows as heavy downpour;
Our valiant archers advanced
To a victory so imminent
Till the aliens we'd adopted
Seized the opportunity
To stab us in the back
So they might rule the land
Alongside the foreign raiders
After our ill-fated defeat.

Part II

The Debauchery of Dictatorial Leadership: A Diary

It was an act of mere
Derogatory
Mean leadership
Mockery
That you opted for daylight
Robbery
To replace the dark night
Burglary
Of a nation dying
Hungry

On Clan Vagrants

Voraciousness rendered the leader less virtuous
Vitiating the morals of the versed to vituperation
The vestige of nationhood shrunk to verbosity
Jargons verily vilifying the vibes of austerity.

He vents human variation on clan vines
Virilities vying along kinship votes
Vindictiveness resonating vilification vices
Making vagabonds and villains vast and vivacious.

Viciousness reigns vibrant in the kinship vein
Venerating the clan virus up to the vertex
Vicars and vigilantes void of virtuoso
Vacuous vampires victimized the public vaults.

They ventilated the ambiance with vendetta
Often venturesome with vulgarity
By their villainy eventually vanished
The verdant brains the land had valued.

Of Alien Eponym(s)

They purported propaganda
On their purity of blood
Blurring all the way
The reality
Of their pedigree.

Can an indefinite
Alien immigrant
Over-flood the earth
With offspring many millions
More than the entire
Nation that adopted him!

Mendacious inscriptions
By imperial abnormality
Obfuscated, undermined,
The indigenes' account of history,
Alluding to academic entombment
Of the aborigines' existence
In the annals of a nation's ancient past.

From a Boatman to a Pedigree: A Somalo-Mythicology

In search of identity status
Above their Africanness
They elevated a strange boatman
To be their original ancestor
Airing a mythical history impossible.

Our forefather came
Alone,
They say,
Across the wild seas
From hinterland Arabia
In a small canoe
That wrecked
On the shores
Of a then bustling Horn
Where he married
A local beauty
So he'd initiate
A phenomenal lineage
That'd absorb into it
The indigenes of the land
Where he was hosted.

Clan Coronation

As a haggard hag in hypnosis
Helen fell in a horrendous hallucination
Hollering in her waffled hangover
For…
Singing a hymn of wild hugger-mugger
As she rose from hysterical hibernation

Helen then puked a misjudgment
Through a mouthful of organism:
I convict the citizens of the rivers
For being hardcore oppressors;
Period!

I duly sign the affidavit that
Only my affinities were affected
Period!

I authorize them for aggression
Upon whose failure they attain
A status of the oppressed
Or those ethnically evaporated
Period!

Nation-Building: An Irony

In a faded dusty wear
Tattered with holes like fishnet
Bunde returns home hungry
Dominating the atmosphere
With heavy stench of cement and lime
A symbol of his nation-building;
He drops down in a squeaky stool
To betray the daunting fatigue
Of a delirious day-long duty
Before a husky voice familiar
From the waves of the wireless
Proudly praised the latest projects
And progress made in the nation.

An air of suspicion and disgust
Got Bunde embellished
Agitating his eons-old anger:
Is the incumbent out of his mind?
Ever since he entered office
I wake up earlier than everyone
Ending my activity later than all
In the dark gloomy evening
Eating once a day a meal meager
Unable to afford a pair of slippers
Or an attire to change this old outfit!

The Nation: Eaters vs. Builders

The engine of my obsolete companion
Struggles to rumble in its unhealthy condition
Both of us weary and fatigue-ridden
In a hot day's duty of late '80s Mogadishu.

I stop for a glass of water to refresh myself
And a gallon to refill my *Dibille* tipper aged
At shacks of kiosks in the vicinity of Hotel Taleh
After taking two or three soothing sips
A colleague cries out to cut short my repose:
"Keep yourself up in quelling your dryness
The couple of us sitting to quench our thirst
May diminish the pillars holding a nation of
Crippled crocodiles caged in this
Glamorous hotel to consume on our sweat."

As I looked at the hotel side I discovered
Cute cars parked clean in every corner
Crowds of army men, courses of functionaries
Consciously committed in fruitless conversation
Over kettles of *caffé nero*, *caffé latte*, and *cappuccino*
Compromising the conscience of work ethics.

Effigies of Tribalism

Dummies impregnated down to the feet
Depict directions of opinions different
Dipping with them tribalism
Into deep earth
As we dream of drawing into one
Diverse ethnicities
A symbol of impossible deviation
From old days' path
When in duels we devastated each other
For clan dignity.

Death, as they say, is attributable
To the destiny of one mortal
Its decreeing rests on the authority
Of the Immortal divine
Who taught us that neither dummies
Nor effigies are due to death;
Disentombing clan dummies
Does worry no man
As death in no way occurred
To my dear clan!

Blessed Revolution: Breadless Nation

Blessed be the revolution of our nation
Our saviour from the subtleties of urban democracy;
The ubiquity of monuments, and control of folklore
Dances by illiterate victory pioneers malfeasant
Reveal the indicators of years of success realized
Remarkable guidelines our ruling junta charted:

Land expropriation, political prisoners,
Kangaroo courts, elite disappearances,
Misappropriation of public funds,
Capital flight and massive brain drain
Mark the great passion for social development.
Our daily praise songs of the nation's father,
The beloved teacher of the breadless nation,
Add footnotes to our appreciation
Of jubilation when we jump in jovial ululation
Not brave enough to break our bond of loyalty
As we build the nation his puppets plundered
And he butchers people who plead with pain;
Yet we're obedient in our participation of
The Starvation Competition he infused
Into the national sport agenda,
Which we *voluntarily* play
In the massive graves
He made our stadium.

The Social Interpretation of XHKS

Fresh from his rural home at sunset
An artist's billboard attracts Aw Caraale
Who scrutinizes the images with anxious look
Admiring the expertise of artwork implemented
But unable to decode the inscription, *XHKS hanoolaado*.

His grandson helps to decode the difficulty as
Xisbiga Hantiwadaagga Kacaanka Soomaaliyeed hanoolaado
An urban dweller's revolutionary jargon wishing
Long life to The Somali Revolutionary Socialist Party.

Dissatisfied with the notion of the revolutionary edifice
Aw Caraale injects a thought-provoking interpretation
Deductively engraving the tone into an inquisitive mode –
Xoow-Hee Ku Siiyey hanoolaadee?
What has XHKS offered you (society)
To deserve your wish for its longevity?

From Camel Rustling to Aid Rustling

My barbaric cousin was born
In a bustling field of beasts
Profuse with illegal property
Stolen booty from the public –
Indeed a child-breeding norm
Inherited from pirating ancestors.

Hence he professes:
State budget and public coffers
Run at perfect par to the clan property
Of which we are the prime beneficiaries
Regardless of the poor citizens
Whose productivity we exploit
To contain them in chronic poverty.

Clan Kiosks

As the dictator's candidate of choice
Nominated on the lunchtime news
Suddenly a figure important
Called a minister prominent;
Wishes and congrats continue
Culminating to uncountable numbers.

Calibrated losers among clan idlers
Quintessential idiots of the kinships
Impregnate the arena with imprudent chatter
Of cabinet kiosks whose keys
Kinfolks were made the custodians of
To cater for the contagion of clan avarice.

"And Boots Too"

The incumbent's frequent trips
Often destinations in Arabia
Left astonishment among the citizenry
Who sang: He who often trots to and fro
On a torrid terrain long and harsh
Tends much to tire the footwear.

Is he back? The daring elderly asked
Announcement stated he's in, answered another
Has he got any aid funds? Asked the sneering citizen
And boots too! Ended the dialogue.

The Overnight Millionaire

In our African homeland
Millionaires are made miraculously
Men who once made a living as
Mini drivers doubling as messengers
Discovered the demonic rhythm
Of a dance called *Clan Disease*
In a society so much dedicated
To demonstrate national dignity.

Before the night waned to dawn
Mini drivers were decreed millionaires
By clan-manufactured miracles
Molding a mix of ideas beyond the metaphor
Of mocking renowned millionaires.

The newly made millionaires malign
Manhandle top managers and ministers.
Our mighty millionaires mapped
Their model of the military police
Mass murderers of the meanest mindset
In minutes shelling mankind like maggots
Before making away with millions
They mugged from the ministries.

The Lady of the Land Cruiser

Lady of the Land Cruiser
Have you a better name
Or any name at all?
Yesterday you drove blue
I called you Ms. Blue
The other day you drove brown
I dubbed you Ms. Brown
Today you man a red one
So I call you Ms. Red
If you're in a white car tomorrow
Won't you be Ms. White?

Lady of the Land Cruiser
How many are your degrees?
How big are the wages
That afford you the affluence?

Alas! Blushed as you were in the bank
That day you sought my assistance
To inscribe for you figures monstrous
On the leaf of your personal check
Insisting I sign it in your place
Though strangers to each other.

Lamentations: A Forsaken Leader

Big promises you made
To die by my side
But you unfulfilled to take pride
During the fratricide;
Most of you sought to hide
A majority made a quick ride.

Bedevilled as you are now in every stride
When all you feel is: what a deride!

Royal Reminiscences

How fast the flip of time!
Wasn't I the absolute authority,
A great incumbent in yesteryears
Ruling under me a nation strong
Autonomous sovereignty enjoyable
Dispatching orders none could ignore
An investment evident of my powers?

Alone in my thoughts unconscious
In the environment of a strange land
Alienated from the world outside
Including the amenities of my authority
Ending up an immigrant without identity
Encapsulated in a hotel room with less accolade.

Today's emergency call empties my soul
Opposition party of my host nation
Enforced the motion for my abdication
Inquiring into the amounts incurred
On the expenditure of my sojourn
In a few days spiralling over a million.
It entails yet another migration murky
Obscure future, unknown destiny,
Anguish at my unfilled aspirations
Foretell of an anomalous omen fastidious
An unremitting blizzard in the backyard.

Part III

Losers and Gainers: Glimpsing Africa's Civil Wars

Some died of blood money
Some died for blood money
Some died in blood money
While some gained blood money
In the "fight against terrorism"
By Uncle Sam's mannerism
Justified with pragmatism
In the Horn's warlordism

War Sonnet

Significance holds
In me to save
My kin serpents:
They send me to battle
Every secret mission
And I am satisfied.
If I cease to sustain
In the salient warfare
Suspend me to be
A sacrificial lamb
So others may survive
To sing my sonnet
Of clan sanctity
And superiority.

The Heartless

He who was born hungry
For human blood
Remains as the heartless
Who hail from *Hawd,*
The inhabitable forests.

He who is habituated
As heinous to hurt
Heeds not harmony
In human dignity
But to cause harm
To innocent humans
Hallucinating the helpless
In every hideous manner.

Armed for Booty

On that fateful day
They ventured fatally
As a team exceeding twenty
To the teeth armed technically
Tipped to attack two herders
Tending a treasure of livestock.

Lo! Scores of tens and twenties
Turbans tightly knotted on the head
Took us from every open turf
Tormenting every hell to break loose
On the arena in their timidless fight
Two of us left lucky to survive
In a typical set of tacit trap!

War Fantasy and Female Warlords

What many a Browning machine gun
We manned along male colleagues madly
We were hiding out in the farmhouses
And dry forests in a remote land unreachable
Firing from muddy trenches during heavy downpour
Ambushing, engaging columns of enemy convoys
Killing senior colonels and commanders-in-chief
In the bombardments of our Best Bride Brigade.

Who said we didn't clinch victory
With the Kalashnikov and the M16;
Who said we didn't climb into the tanks
Or the armored personnel carriers,
The field artillery that rocked the earth?
Who said we didn't launch the anti-aircraft missiles?

Who else could afford the espionage operations
We executed under cover of our exquisite veils
When in the streets of Mogadishu men often
Fell easy prey in targeted enemy territories?

From feeding the clan army to
Physical fighting in the frontline
We functioned far too well
Than one could fathom from our felony!

Though our fame as the *forsaken females*
Fitted to down-fume our ferociousness
The fantasy of killing felt fair and fine with us
Finally honoring our female warlords!

Exodus into the Wilderness

First in the west
Then in the east
Later in the north
Last in the south.

Unleash the artillery
Enemy out of the hideouts
Aeroplanes in the air
Armed men in arrays
Automatic rifles ruinous
Citizens caught in
Chaotic cross-firing
Sickly smell of gunpowder
Confusion, frustration
Giant salvos jostled homes
Leaving dozens deaf and dumb;
Hand grenades were hurled
Huge hugger-mugger ensued
Past the doorstep lay tens deceased
Fed on by millions of fat maggots.
Restless survivors escaped into a wasteland
Through audacious expedition
Sharing the wilderness with wildlife
Than sharing word with humans wild.

Killing a Close Kin

The Kalashnikov cocked
Coughing out bits of hot copper
Freshly spilled blood
Covered the cute car outside
Crowds of people keenly observe
The young killer in combat gear
Carrying the corpse calmly aside
In complacent admiration of its keys
That caused him to kill a caring uncle.

The Grave-looting Game

Grief-stricken relatives perspiring at sunrise
Paying painful homage to a dear one who
From rocket shells the night before retired from life.

While reciting the invocation verses
Before interring the corpse in its rest place
In the horizon appeared an army anonymous.

Rumbling bullets shimmered into the crowd
Adding more anxiety to the stampede
As the dead was abandoned at the graveyard.

Upon returning after resumption of calm
Indeed in the coffin the body still lay intact
Only alienated from its tomb by another corpse
Ending up a victim again after death
Of a grave-looting game by an armed gang.

Kinship Loyalty

Beyond significance
It is so sacrosanct to save
My serpentine kin;
Send me to battle
Every secret mission;
If I cease to sustain
In salient warfare
Suspend me to be
A sacrificial lamb.

A Proud Killer

Born hungry
For human blood
A hideous hawk
Hailing from heartlessness
Heinous to hurt.

He heeds nothing
But to cause harm
To innocent humans,
Hallucinating the helpless
In every hateful way.

An Ill-fated Attack

A team exceeding twenty
To the teeth armed technically
Tipped to attack two herders
Holding tangible treasure of wealth
Taking them to task turbulent
In a timidless fight.

Lo! Scores of tens and twenties
Turbans tightly knotted to the head
Took us from every open turf
To break loose a tormenting hell
As the try for wealth tempted us into
A typical set of tacit trap!
Two of us survived to tell
The tale of that fateful day.

"It Needs Bold Men Today!"

Heavy gunfire deafened the environment
Premonition of the unprecedented baffled
The dozen or so skinny young warriors
Who fell in disarray of team organization.

From his bed their ailing intrepid leader states:
"Under-equipped boys less than ten or eleven
Leave little to stand for the thunder blast roaring –
Oh! How today's burden needs men enough!"

The groaning of the guns intensified
Precursor of untameable enemy closing in:
Victory is unlikely in our situation
Evacuate me right away, snarled the commander.

The touching words traumatized the frantic
Militia who paced out in the open with
A piece of white cloth tied around their heads
As a token of bravery on the path to death;
A signal shot burst to take up positions
Two teams dispersed to left and right
The middle column responding and retreating
Blasts of gun powder pounding unabated
Exchanges of bazookas and rockets sprawled
The sickly commander crawled to the door
To die a manly death: fighting,
Than die in bed, as a coward *hiding*.

Soon the boys returned home
Fantasized at the height of joy
Stomping in the rhythm of folk chant
Hollering to a hyper hymn of fiesta:
"Oh! How today's burden got men enough!"

Confidential: From Mogadishu to Abidjan

So abruptly... heh!
Those who hypnotized Taylor in a hunt down
Entered me into the ICC book of culprits
Over the death of thousand Ivorians unknown
Omitting those eliminated from my side
As undesirables invalidated from earth.

The astounding knowledge in me
The average wisdom I employed
Did not attract Uncle Sam to the options
I laid in the academic resolutions I offered;
Instead, they abducted me against my wish
Airlifting me in front of Africa to the ICC arena
Before indicting my innocent wife;
What is your opinion, experienced warlords
Of Africa's Northerly Horn?

Balaayaa ka dhacday! Hell broke loose!
When you sought the resort to reasoning
You spoilt every opportunity in your docket
By ignoring Uncle Sam as the elderly authority
Of evil, all things irredentist, irrational.

Understanding Uncle Sam needs not academic intellect,
We liquidated away from life over half a million humans
And went scot-free with it we engaged him once or twice
In the '90s; only God knows what happened!
From those misunderstandings emerged this bilateral treaty:
We implicate a few youths and radical Islamists
To affiliation with Al Qaeda and unknown dissidents
Scare the sh** out of him: that another attack could be
Imminent on the shores of the US in view of
The reliable information we access from
The local agents of Al Qaeda. And Uncle Sam, scared to death,
Offered us monthly stipends in hundreds of thousands

Every end month, for incriminating others against him
As we seek his consent to disincriminate us – reciprocally –
Of all the atrocities we committed over the last two decades,
Understanding Uncle Sam needs not academic intellect.

Part IV

Leadership Lost: The Somali Transitional Administrations

The burst of whispers
Into the height
Left us frozen
In our fright:
That
Lucifer courted them
At night
To constitute the state
At day's light,
Convening them
Into horrible fight
That blew public coffers
Into flight

The *Ideal* Warlord!

My way, or their way?
Who makes the real law?
Memos signed in the middle of the night?
Or the mindless adamant in my persona?

Monies were spent on mean delegates
Seeking recourse from harsh life at home
Celebrating honeymoons in the hotel rooms
Folks lacking hope to harness a nation.

I'm here to hobble head-on
Every noble initiative named nationalism;
Either I gain, or it ends a zero-sum game
No matter the consequences I'll meet
For the obstinacy installed in me.

Make a memo of understanding with me
The master of the marauding militia
Who man much military equipment
In most of the major townships.

Parliamentarian Pugilists

The criteria for our parliamentarians
In the TFG charter in quotations
Informs qualities high in notions
In the art of Kung Fu and Karate
Kickboxing, wrestling, and conquering
The cowards seeking cabinet posts
Corner each other along the corridors
Unleash fast jabs followed by uppercuts
Bare-knuckled blows in athletic styles
Until the body of the weak is bundled
Over the podium with brilliant maneuver.

A Cult Called Clan Cabinet

In his briefcase
Carrying a portfolio
As beautiful a souvenir
As a bouquet of roses
Albeit its blossom not beyond
The borders of the bag itself
Though a belligerent tribe
Bellows it out as a pride
A potent membership to
A cult called cabinet
Assigned to cater
For the clan compatriots.

Betrayed by a passion
For clan politics
The bouquet briefcase
Borders poignant promises
Bulging with pride bolted
On merely plastered pillars
Breaking from inside
Due to poor workmanship.

Modern Minister's Confession

Over the past two decades and a while
Us Somalis sprouted into two Diaspora entities
Adeegte: He who serves himself to public property and
Aqoon-lafadhiye: He who loafs around with knowledge
I opted to settle for *Adeegte* for self-service.

I'm an immigrant enrolled
In several countries around
At the end of every month
Or even a fortnight term
I wait in a dole queue long
To claim state alimony.

As an expert in the art as *Adeegte*
I also squandered a cabinet post
In my country of origin
To access the unlimited funds
Entering our nation from outside
To extend our cabinet income.
Aqoon-lafadhiye, though erudite,
Is sitting idle to educate others
While earning one income small
Every period of two fortnights –
After insurance bill and taxes axed
Barely earning enough for a living.

Kiosks, Coffee Shops, and Corner Garages

Our Transitional Federal Charter
Adopted recent changes further
Vital for our sovereign state
That Mogadishu despite the capital
Cabinet meetings as well as
Crucial legislative conferences
Could be held in the coffee shops
And small kiosks in Kenya's
Squalid Eastleigh quarters.

For reasons of convenience, comfort, and class
As clarified in the clauses of the canon charter:
Coffee shops for cabinet meetings
Kiosks for legislative conferences
Corner garages for the committee congress.

Today and Tomorrow

If tomorrow does promise no rains
Any better than our today's droughts
Won't the dark of the night cast plagues
Of malice into the new dawn's plights?
Among beloved brothers and sisters
When hatred engulfs the hearts --
Won't prudence vow communal deviations
From the details of the social norms
That border personal ideals
With natural realities?

Part V

A Limerick on Lame Academic Leadership

Oh, Mr. Guardian!
Your proliferation
Of a top brass inept
Led to the celebration
Of staff moral decimation
As enviable glorification –
Hence the unethicality vibrant
In your leadership malignant
Though only I can state it
In the crowded open market

The Poet: A Leader

As the marine is bequeathed
With miracles so magic
And heavens take pride
With beauties magnificent
As the night stars and moon
Promise another day and destiny
And the wise query fairness
In the balance of a judgment passed
The poet engraves on the memory
A textual contour of the theme
Portrayed from the conscious mind
And the searching eyes and soul
Of the intrinsic social emotion
Entertained with apocryphal talk
Entrapped in an airtight realm
Intrigued by long lost aspiration.

Moral Decimation

Over a span of eons
Your allergy to ethics
Augmented the ailments

The torment of aimlessness
Imbibed in the appeals
Of your emptied souls
Abrogated the ideals
Of our academic excellences

When eighty percent of our harvest
Earn less than a projected eminence
Anger grips the entire land
But the two top cooks burst
Shamelessly into laughter
And the untouched, turban-clad
Topmost chef takes tens
Of compatriot kitchen cabinet to joyride
While two toadying tobacco-teasers team up
To turn over the outcome top down
For the table of our earnings to read
"Only twenty percent drop-out"

Charlatans' Chicanery: A Poetic Barb

To the poor old boy of the Nile Valley who sounded convinced that colonialism had helped Africa.

When I gather momentum without goof or gibber
I glow the verse to gravitate into gradual height
So I grab the gadfly and gauge his glitch good
To spill his garbage galore in the African griots' gala
Rather than gawk and let go of one galvanized with graft.

A gangling African ganger's gibberish language
Got me to gape at him in gimmick disgust with gloom
On how he gurgled a gargantum account of colonial glee
Garnishing imperialism as great achievement Africa gained
From its grisly gang-raping by the Western ghosts!
Such is the decayed grain the continent got:
A go-between gob, glib-tongued gossiper
Good-for-nothing gofer in global terms
Colonial gardener elevated as super gatekeeper
Gormless guide and graduate in gift-wrapping
Master of grand jugglers ghastly in every gathering.

Woe to thee whom society cursed as:
Genetic germ to the genre African genus
Guru in the art of goading the good-hearted
Goody-two-shoes genuflecting for the pseudo grandee
So they may gate-crash you into a leadership gazebo
To gerrymander the goalposts that gauge morality.

A Tactless Toady

Wild whispers went around
Waging war of words on
The timid tactical survivors
Within the turf of their tummies
A cursed lot beaten of any edifying talent.

Our community calls them
Toadying culprits tranquil
With minuscule titbits,
Tie-clad thieves who take
A tiny ticket or twenty-fiver
For which they topple
The towering traits and token
Of our top-notch center of talent.

The Incompetent

Let me lampoon the worthless Luddite
With the lancet of the luminous lines:
Laggard laagers in long lullaby
Lackadaisical lizards limping
Low-level lackeys lagging behind
Loathsome lapdogs lapping for largesse
Landscaping for lucre as the lynchpin of life
Liquidating a learning hub into lame duck
Lewd bumpkins of letdown to the literati.

My look of things lured me hence to state:
Didn't they see how –
Loopholes lay large enough in your leadership?
Leading to the description of –
Lotus-eaters in the locality of illiterate lords.
Didn't I hear society say: the mean don't grow
Above licking boots for gain of little opportunity? –
Before our octogenarian chief attributed them:
Lumberjacks lowering the head down to the loin
Less learned in the logics of leadership, though
Lumped into a top lacuna without a ladder
Like the lustreless loungers in ancient lores
Who took leisure amid a looming landslide!

Nefarious Nexus

Strong and weak leaderships exist everywhere, in every profession, and academia is not an exception. This verse is dedicated to all men and women academics who at some point in their professional life felt oppressed, frustrated or marginalized for one reason or another by the powers that be in their respective institutions.

As a self-proclaimed property
Nobility does not warrant
Noblesse oblige, for
Self-respect negates to be nestled
In the nexus of a nefarious one
Long forsaken by society.

Prudence once betrayed by prowess
May play proxy to poetic justice, but
As when boastful belligerents get beaten
Procrastinators may bear the blame
When breach of promises becomes virulent
Scholars may place the guilt on wicked leadership.

Pitiable Leadership: So Noxious a Premonition

On that day, like the era of the Arab Spring,
Academics advanced to express the ailments
That amputated the endurance of their tolerance
As they uttered out and loud in front of inhabitants
Astonished, abysmally emotional:

Unacademicality embraced unethicality
Unethicality embellished immorality
Immorality ushered in hypocriticality
Hypocriticality hinged its fate on vanity
Vanity celebrated academic unethicality.

When barren patches breed no more
Like ponds of water in drought and thirst
Psyches empty of reason glorify unjust
Promising no meaningful remedy to adore
Except the soul's violent persistence to exist
In minds and morals decayed, defunct.

Our current observation alludes to
Eruptions of evil in the environment
Infections by wolves worthless, inept
Elbowing the astute in favor of ethnicity
So they insist on the application
Of a pedagogy severely a calamity;
A status quo horrendously insanity
Stressed much as appalling, a pity!

Analysis of our observation entails
Academics under oppression
Unendurable commotion
Antagonistic suppression.
If unabated the frustration,
Promptly with precaution,
It may entice invincible petition

As an ultimate consolation
That ejects as a solution
The incumbent in desolation
Desperation, dilapidation
Derogation, denunciation.

Aside of the lurid lamentation
We assure our loyalty
To the lovely ones we lactate
Inside the lecture hall.

Disadvantage: Dichotomous Diction

We own no leverage
In our habitat Disadvantage
Where we live under bondage;
Because in Disadvantage
The elderly wear the bandage
After inflicting others the damage.

Once upon in Disadvantage
They endorsed sixty as the band age
That one should quit Disadvantage.

One day, a senior delivered a message
Asking a tenant to hit the passage
For touching the ceiling of the band age
Though the carrier of the message
Had a decade ago crossed the limit age.

Lo! How that messenger in our Disadvantage
Is mean to cover many a mileage
Till we pay him the final homage!

Till We Became Unseen!

We followed the decree
That everything should be
Unseen
So we created the vocabulary quiz
As an assessment based on the
Unseen
And the comprehension quiz
Had to follow suit and be
Unseen
Weekly tests and unit tests
Should reflect the same as
Unseen
Paving the way for the exit test
To conclude all assessments of the
Unseen
Till our efforts and motivations
Were tossed into the trash and made
Unseen

Reshuffles, Stunts, and Servants

A vigilant insider
Is never fooled
By the tricks
Of the stunt master
No matter
What the perceived
Magic he performed.

And as the Arabic adage goes,
Sometimes:
The likelihood of the coming rains
May be predictable from the clouds.

Can reallocations
Within hamlets
Therefore
Caution us as forewarnings
For disturbing endings
Looming for the chefs
In the royal courts?

Languish without Lament

In the wake of his authority
The incumbent felt
Like an enormous *angel*
In the environs of heavens
Built in his castle,
The base of the beauty
That portrays his prowess.

He saw with more eyes
Than other humans;
He heard every word
Through the auditory organs
Of the inauspicious spies
He installed among us
Innocent interlocutors.
He admonished all to regard
A state of expressionlessness:
Look but do not see
Listen but do not hear
Languish but do not lament.

When the torrential rains
From societal remorse
Shook the foundations
Of the castle into fractures
Cracks, leaks, flakes
Then came the loud calls
To contain the king's courts;
With comfort we cast our claims:
We look but we don't see
We listen but we don't hear
When you languish we don't lament!

Of Primates and the Boat: A Poetic Drama
Episode I
Sanura, the Rejects, and Desert Seal

Admiral Desert Seal took over Sanura,
A fast-sailing craft in the summer
Which sustained the hardships of winter
Spring, fall, and the damnedest
Of wild monsoon weathers
Till due to his dangerous daftness
He siphoned the admiralship
To an ineligible old ape from
The environs of the white river.

Alongside came another
An easy-going mandrill,
A sibling of the ape,
To operate under the command
Of a lousy chimp labeled among
The rejects of Uncle Sam's offspring;
His amorphous errands included
To oversee the chores
Of an incapable brute,
Immensely ineffectual,
Though imported from
Elizabeth's Isle.

Episode II

A Call Too Desperate

When sailors surmised the high seas
As symptoms of sad endings
For the sail of pretty Sanura
The senior primates
Suggested impractical solutions
That made Sanura unsailable.

The ensuing anger of the sailors
Spelled out sour afflictions
Of a long-enduring curse.
Gloom of spirits unheard of
Eliminated a cunning couple
Into high seas home-bound
Humiliated with devilish haunt.

Then cruel waves turned turbulent
Tossing Sanura into spins
That took the tactless three weary,
An overwhelm of gnawing anxiety
In the overheated engine-room,
An alarming SOS aloud:
Shutters!
Cracks!
Floods!

Episode III

The Sinking: May the Lord Save Sanura!

A besieged three began the blame game;
Seal bombarded his pithless aides
With baleful taunts unbearable
Then burst at the bashed, belittled creatures:
Poor performance, bogus credentials
Both of you sacked with no benefits!

Feeling a betrayed perpetrator,
Seal pulled a telegraphed paper
From Sanura's parent owner;
His period as the principal
Was brought to blushing end
Burgeoning the pustules
Of the bad omen perturbing
His ballooning potbelly!

Before airing his plea for pardon
Against the board's bashing decision
The potential saviors had parted ways
With the three beleaguered primates
Sailing off in the last safety boat
Singing a sorrowful song
In soothing smiles:
"Hi De Hi, Hi De Ho!"

The Unethical

Preaching what is not practiced
Burgles the bosom and boosts
Bankruptcy in brain-thinking,
Belittling one's self-respect
Also bruising old bonds bilateral.

Boasting and prattling big
Do not in them portray
Potent policies or power,
While beholding no pale of truth
Later blushes the bogus with
The bleak burden of shame.

As the ironic elder informed me:
The baleful place of the perjurer,
The breacher of the promised word,
Rests at the base and bottom of things
Which pulps off the pillars of integrity
Bred and borne in the heart of the betrayed.

Part VI

Dialogue of the Dead

How dreadful reimaging
The evils I committed
In conceit when I enacted
Injustice a life prevailing
In the state I reigned
With insanity people deemed
Democracy 'a little' duped
By clan advisors daunting
In every respect damaging

Arguments from the After-world: A Drama

Immediately after accommodated into his resting place
The argumentative newcomer yells aloud
Raising complaint over insufficient space
Unable to stretch sticky legs curved as a co ne
Attacking neighbors absorbed in the depth of fun

The familiar voice disturbed a deep sleeper
Astonished by the unexpected odd visit of
The comer and his complaint unprecedented!
Cautious listening clarified the question
The comer was his colleague, an army colonel

W. Peace be upon you, comrade Colonel
Calmness is a condition sacred in these quarters

X. Without chaos the course of the journey to here wouldn't count;
But who called for your conciliation to this conflict?

W. Your critical complaint caused the earth quivering
Awakening uncountable souls in earnest calm

X. Expansion of territory is my all-the-way aim
Unless you already appropriated all the land

W. Our earlier expropriation should be adequate
And abstain from evil doing in the approach to Accounting Day

X. When you ate alone prime areas ashore the rivers
You assigned me duties overseas to your advantage

W. Later you ambushed my authority and ousted me
Squandering alone the arable land in inter-riverine Somalia

Upon hearing the dialogue
Skeletal youths stood still in supplication
Orphans and the elderly hands up in the air
Widows dressed in white, praying in prostration

Asking Almighty the abrupt accommodation
Of the new immigrant away from the environment

       Angels reporting to Allah about the rowdy comer
       Returned restlessly with rocks of red embers
       And huge metal rods of replenishable hellfire
       With harmful spikes stud on the head like horns;
       Hallucinating punishment ensued and heavy hammering
       The harrowing cries of the heartless comer were heard
       Hurtful to the ear of the heavenly souls in every horizon
Lo, he hit back with hard kicks harmless in the heavenly world
Before a crossfire of the hellish spikes were hauled in his head
       Opening up holes in his heart with harpoons
       His heartfelt call for clan help remained heedless
       His unsaintly vows for heinous retaliation rampant
       Received him the rage of God and many reinforced rocks
       The ruins of his rotten soul left to repose for recovery

       W. Superstars before you have suffered here
       Certainly suffocating their hopes for mercy

       X. I'll seek solace and summon a sophisticated army
       Surmounting my attackers into ceaseless subjugation
       Their secret hideout will not save them any the situation
       Once my superior technicals send soundless rockets;
       Sufficiently equipped boys seeking no surrogates
       Will succeed to severely subdue the enemy's sanctuary

       W. These angels operate under Almighty's instructions
       The idea of attacking the invincible agents of Allah
       Ordained to be invisible, utterly sounds insane
       Especially old army men like us who established
       Undesirable records in our early first life
       Arrogantly avoiding adherence to Allah's word

       X. Are we in another world other than that early one?
       What is your evidence that we're in the afterlife?
Or, is your allusion to scare me again for your advantage?

W. Armored escorts are unavailable for your aid
Your immediate engagement by Allah's angels
Proves assurance to the extinction of your earthly authority
X. Is Allah the other man in authority in this world?

W. Allah is not a man, but the Almighty authority everywhere!

X. Does another authority exist except you, me, and America?

W. *Allahu Akbar!* Allah is the Omnipotent authority of all!

X. Invite him to an ad hoc meeting among the three of us
To achieve an agreement of mutual understanding
Then we amass stealthily our undefeatable armies
Assault *Afar-Irdood*, the inter-riverine, up to the gates of *Adale*
Assail our opponents including Ethiopia and America across the Atlantic
After victory we streamline angels and all armies against him
As overthrowing him at once will usher in our authority
Eventually ordaining the two of us overall lords in every world

W. The excruciating agony I encountered to achieve that ideology
Annihilated my slight opportunity for Allah accepting my apology:
Observant archangels tossed at me taboos of curses taunting
Torturing me traumatically till my skin was tattooed, tattered.

Incessant pandemonium from the outside
Accrued into the ears of the old army men

X. Theatrical animation or a world in its actual sense?

W. Spirits of those we oppressed in the old world.

X. Are they pledging allegiance to our authority?

W. In solemn supplication for our ultimate extinction
Also a prediction of intolerable punishment ensuing
Against each of their words we're entitled to suffer
The equivalent to eighty-eight years' flogging

X. And what was I attacked for a while ago?

W. It was an introduction: a welcome offer!

X. Only introduction, all that I underwent!

W. Only an intro, if I know it only too well!

X. An attempt to escape?

W. Unthought-of; absolutely impossible!

X. What's our fate like in this odd world of eternal life?

W. Eternality of all types of punishment unknown to us!

X. And the angels always come invisible?

W. And invincible, too!

The Unexpected Encounter

Y. In my terms the public enjoyed
Peace and multi-party progress
Bourgeoisies and penny lovers
Had their pages closed permanently
Clan politics and tribal bigwigs
Both out of business during my politburo
Till neocolonial pedants like you
Politicized kinship paradigms
With bag-loads of money
And promises for posts

Z. The basis for African politics
Praises clan partnership;
Pedants portray power of knowledge
Unlike political bankrupts like you
Put in power by fascist bosses
To plainly promulgate in parliament
Bestial colonial purposes
Blocking motions for peasant rights
Seeking presidential approval for
Litigation on land properties looted.

Y. Point of clarification, please;
Parcels of the land properties
Appropriated by the colonial power
Part of which I, too, purchased from Bono[1]
Belong not to the Somali peasantry
Who practice pastoralism, but
Bantu *Jareer*, the *Beyla-sanbuur*[2]
Whose property and as a people are
Partitioned by our hidden bylaws
Not to benefit from the prerogatives
Of my presidential powers and privileges

Z. Which of Plato's books purveys the portrayal
That your Bantu policy bears no basis for clan politics?
By far the public proposes you as the primary perpetrator

Potently paving the path for the political oppression
Purporting the socio-economic poverty of the Bantu peasants

Y. As a political personality I'm proud to bear the burden of blame
Particularly in protecting the interests of Paulo, the powerful
Also the planners holding the potential to boost my portfolio
Prefabricating my presidential post prior to its parliamentary approval
Thus promoting me from barber and bartender to president of state

1. Bono is Italian name and represents colonial master
2. *Beyla-sanbuur:* is a derogatory word which means broad-nosed African; it is used for the
Bantu Jareer people in Somalia and for any other black African with a broad nose.

Z. Somalis were in subtle mood searching for sovereignty
It sufficed their sentiment to sign to sadist sounding sanctimonious
Not seeing the soiling and sabotage under the surface
The severe side you took in the soppy *Leylkase* saga!

Y. The senior staff surrounding the soppy *Leylkase* saga,
Solely the two main solicitors supervising the situation,
Are superlative subscribers and supporters from your clan self-same;
Selling me as a sacrificial lamb surmises my being the soft side
Secrets unknown to Somali-*weyn* now deeply sink my situation
Circumstances secluded from human sight now surface atop
Serious complaints from the *sanbuur* and the sage submerged
The submission of my case and the succor I so much longed for
Suiting my stable suspension from the site of the sinless
Summoning me as among the morally seized
Those to be suspended into the simmering fire of hell

Z. I'm suggested safe with the Somalis but certainly save the *sanbuur*
We selfishly sanctioned their suppression for our self-satiation
Superimposing secured segregation against their society
Subordinating them effectively from sources of economy
We suffocated the salience of their right at the legislative circles
So many of us perpetually suffer for the sins against society.

Part VII

A Limn of the Looting Spree: A Presidential Decree

To those who exalt leadership from the distorted premise of 'willing seller, willing buyer.'

...And we insisted
As many before us admitted
That we weren't duped
When we created
A history that wasn't
For one who himself wasn't
What we exalted
Him of, which he wasn't,
Albeit all he *was* was wasn't

The Decreed Army Man

The unamendable decree
Declares the diverse duties
Delegated to officers of the *nobility*:
The top brass in the army
Of the notable nobility
Report late in office
With a duty of drinking tea and coffee
Departing office at their earliest desire
On condition that they do so
Only after a drop at the fuel depot
And the department of finance
Then drive to downtown
To date drunkard dames dearly
For dinner, wild drink and dance
Or debate over debris of Qaat
During which to discuss
How the department head
Could dignify their promotion
And deem approval *tout de suite*
Their demand for more dollars
During their next departure
To Denmark or Denver
To decrease the drastic stress
Due to the heavy duty at home.

The Decreed Civil Servant

As the backbone of the nation
The decree decorates this nation builder
With privileges and rights of his wish,
Unlimited visits to the coffers
With prevalent conditions that
Visits be as frequent as possible
That his personal advantages supersede
National goals and interests
As much so as clan or kinship projects
While not compromising the standard ethics
Governing clan representation and
Participation in the cooking pot
Of Maandeeq's delicious meat;
The more effectively he executes these
The more guarantee the promotion
With all types of due processes waived;
The faster the frequencies
Of visiting the coffers unaccompanied,
The larger the pockets and bags

The Decreed Businessman

Operating licenses will be
Withdrawn from the idiot trader
Reporting losses and other strains
While knowing our service to him
Stays sacrosanct and unbendable,
Let alone broken by hammers
Of jealousy or rivalry by other clans,
Knowing the availability of funds
Both in unlimited loans and
In grants especially designed
To protect his business
Boost his personal income
The arrogant behavior
To engage, slap any human
At will in the town streets
Solemnly equipped with powers
Above the entirety of the laws of the land
Even exempting him from the hassle
Of repaying his statutory loans whatsoever
By daringly decorating his status with
The *ka-aamus* letter we signed
That none can hold him responsible
For whatever funds he received
From the financial houses we set up for him.

Prayers for the Decreed Incumbent

Elaborated, this decree affirms
Head of state as an anointed outsider
From the affairs of the administration;
It empowers his lack of intervention
In time of acute need for advice
In the cabinet or at legislative level;
It consolidates his authority to sway
Any complaints against colonial Italy
As forwarded by the indigenes
The affected amongst the peasantry.

This presidential prerogative purports
His legality to purchase plantations
All properties the colonialists plundered
From the Bantu Jareer peasantry.
It further declares him an impotent player
In the provocations of businesses in parliament
Party issues pertaining to public interest
Despite placing him as principled power authority
With passion for the entire public,
One who pledges loyalty to the people
Apparently of two clans important
As plainly stated in the pages
Of Gassim's volume of politics;
Say Amen –
Amen!
That presidential power of attorney
Be effectively practiced
By his potent brothers-in-law
Who preset the profanity of state property
To ostracise the learned brand
From performing in the public sector –
Amen!
That the weaknesses conferred upon him
By his utter lack of wisdom

So scholars may daringly (mis)ensconce it
As apt neutrality of even leadership –
Amen!
May arduous efforts be exerted
Efficaciously, in the concoction
Of an exalted, artificial biography
That obscures his inner hypocrisy –
Amen!
May his ineptitude alliterated in these prayers
Fizzle out of the aerated biographer's eyes –
Amen!
May the public remain blinkered
To the incumbent's predilections –
Amen!
May his ingenuousness
Endure him as Italy's blessed puppet –
Amen!
May the Bantu-Jareer be oppressed
Alongside the Yibir and Tumaal
As expressionless humans
Invalidated, incapacitated forever –
Amen!
May the literati stay numb
Over the entirety of his undoing –
Amen!
May his progeny benefit plenty
From pro-colonial *Borsa di Studio** –
Amen!
May his in-laws emerge blameless
Over the oft played-down *Leylkase* plot –
Amen! Amen! Amen!
May the expropriated Bantu Jareer land
He *inherited* from his colonialist colleagues
Enjoy nationwide legitimacy –
Amen! Amen! Amen!
May the stolen *hal booli* she-camel*
Give birth to *nirig xalaal* legitimate calf –
Amen! Amen! Amen!
May we ordain him with affluence

In the annals of our national history
As the holy man unholy –
Amen! Amen! Amen!

* *Borsa di studio:* Italian phrase for scholarship
*From the Somali adage '*hal xaaraan ah nirig xalaal madhasho*'
meaning – a stolen she-camel can never beget a *xalaal*/kosher calf.

www.ingramcontent.com/pod-product-compliance
Lightning Source LLC
Chambersburg PA
CBHW070927160426
43193CB00011B/1595